D0616461

INSEMINATION AT HOME: EXACTLY WHAT MY WIFE AND I DID TO GET ME PREGNANT

Amanda Ford

CONTENTS

PREFACE

My hope for this whole book is to help you, to empower you. It's to give back because I was given my whole family, my whole life. There is so much information out there, there's so much help, so much research. There are also a lot of questions, a lot of contradictions. What I couldn't really ever find is a play by play of what I could or should be doing, confirmation that my best was the best I could do. What I really wanted to know is how exactly someone went through the process. So, if you're wondering the same thing, I'm here with you. This isn't a book for lesbians or a book for couples or for singles. This is a book for anyone thinking about doing an insemination at home, anyone looking for a friend, anyone looking for someone to say "hey, I've been there." I'm not a doctor or an expert. All I know is what I did. I hope you'll be able to use my research and my experience in your journey.

INTRODUCTION

Besides the occasional dreams about women in my early teens, a brief love affair my junior year of college with a woman, and my ever present interest in potentially touching a breast someday, I had always dated guys until I turned 28.

Ahhh 28, the year I broke up with my very stable boyfriend. He's the one I started dating after my very unstable boyfriend swung me off my feet and dumped me twice at airports around the world. That's neither here nor there and unlikely to be the reason one night I downloaded Tinder and when they asked me my preference I selected women not men.

I always said that I would be disappointed and would feel like I didn't live my best life if I had never explored a relationship with another woman. I had always been a fly by the edge of my seat, doing what I want, when I want, the kind of gal who leaps before looking.

That night as I picked out the pictures that would establish me in the dating women scene (a picture of me with the monkey from "The Hangover", me caught conveniently in a jump in the middle of a beautiful Thai beach from my year abroad, etc...) I wasn't thinking of anything other than touching breasts, and dabbling in a plethora of women that would be the next chapter of my crazy life. Well as luck would have it I was pretty good at picking up women and by the end of the night I got some numbers and went to bed dreaming about all that was to come.

I wasn't worried about my family's acceptance, my friends' understanding, what having a family would consist of, or the road that would soon become my journey. None of it actually ever crossed my mind. While I was busy galavanting around with the woman that would become my wife it hit me, slowly but surely, that there were hundreds of things I never thought of.

I never thought my Dad would say he wasn't going to go to Thanksgiving because I'd be bringing my new girlfriend home, or that my girlfriend's parents wouldn't talk to her for nearly a year after she too told them for the first time she was dating a woman. I didn't take into consideration that our fights would be more intense, more passionate, and much more complicated than fights I'd had with other people I've dated.

But through all of the ups and all of the downs I never thought about the obstacles family planning might bring us. Two women having a child never crossed my mind as an obstacle, challenge, nothing...I usually assume that things will work out. But how does one exactly get pregnant when her spouse is a woman and how much does it cost? I wondered.

So, like with most other big questions I have in life I hit the internet in search for how I'd get pregnant in the future. I found sperm online. I could order sperm and then somehow I would put it in my body!? For some reason this was the strangest thing. I never even considered this option. All I had ever heard of or assumed existed was going to a doctor and having them figure it all out. I scrolled through a pretty sketchy website selling sperm, absolutely amazed, clicking on anything and everything. People actually do this? But the more I looked into it the more normal it seemed. Why couldn't people order sperm? You basically can order everything else.

I screenshotted that first website and sent it to my now wife. You can order sperm online! And when she responded, I'm not sure if she was as elated as I was but more so approached it in the reserved way I had at the beginning. I jump in headfirst. My wife cautiously dips her feet in, really taking in everything. By this point I was already ordering the sperm, inseminating, basically I was already pregnant in my mind. But I didn't know the half of it, what insemination consisted of.

What inseminating entailed for me is doing everything the best I could do it. Tracking, eating healthy, getting well, using the right whositswhatsits, doing everything I could to accomplish pregnancy because when I do things, I fully do them, committing, immersing and almost driving myself to a heart attack stressing about every little detail. Don't stress they say, it'll stop you from getting pregnant...it didn't.

Over the course of five months my wife and I did three inseminations at home. My first was in December and when we tried we were both overly optimistic, relied almost solely on apps to track and were under the impression whatever was meant to be was meant to be. That time there was just no way I would have gotten pregnant because of our lack of knowledge.

The second time, in March, I had been tracking a lot more closely, I was eating healthy, going to the chiropractor and the acupuncturist regularly and bringing spirituality into my everyday life. We were confident but still I second guessed myself and the tracking I was doing. I didn't go with my gut but instead went with what apps were showing me.

The third time I took charge. I ate the meals I had researched, I walked every morning. I went to the chiropractor and acupuncturist. I did my essential oil routines. I tracked with my own calendars. We used the tools available including the ovulation tests, the apps, we even went to a fertility center the week before our pregnancy test tested positive.

The biggest difference? I listened to myself. I knew I was doing the best I could do. I felt good, I was healthy. I was tracking what I needed to track and listening to my body. So, when it came time and lots of signs pointed to "not the right time to inseminate" but my body, heart and soul said it was, I went with it.

STEP 1 : GETTING STARTED

You're Getting Pregnant How!?

The number one lesson I wish I had learned earlier? Don't let any-one psych you out from the process of at home insemination.

I never heard of at home insemination before I needed it and searched for it. Then I found this beautiful option and almost everyone dumped on it. Does it seem a little out there? Yes, of course. It seems too good to be true. No doctors, no pills, no shots, just order your sperm and inseminate, that's it. Obviously there's more that goes into it but it is the most natural process after a man and a woman having sex.

Most people probably won't ask how you're doing it, or when you get pregnant how you did it. I've noticed it's pretty much assumed that you used IVF. That's what people hear about, shots and struggles and relationships on the cliff because of the hor-mones and stress and breakdowns. ICI, it makes people close down. What is it? Isn't there only one way? Your wife does what? You get the sperm in the mail?

But most people don't ask questions at all, even most of my closest friends shied away from the details. Is it disgust, worry, ignorance, are they scared to offend us or look stupid? I have no idea. My only guess is that because people don't know about it, it doesn't seem possible, it doesn't seem safe, it doesn't seem like it would work, and if it did? Well, if it did that would be weird, un-known, unsettling.

My therapist of 17 years asked if I was flushing away my money down the toilet but assured me that there are plenty of other ways that people like me could get pregnant. She told me to look at all the options, and what about adoption? Maybe I should go to a doctor, they could probably give me other ways to do things. Luckily she knew plenty of people that used IVF and got pregnant, had I looked into that?

My family members said go to a doctor, they know what they're doing. When it didn't work once and then it didn't work the second time they were convinced, this was only a job for a doctor. How could we know what we were doing? Had I looked into IVF? A lot of people have been successful with that, no one actually knew any of those successful people but they'd heard of them.

There were many "well if that doesn't work you could always..." Mind you all of these people had no idea what we were going through, what the options actually were, what the process we were currently going through was. Some would probably say they were just trying to be supportive in the only way they knew how, and those people would probably be right but it doesn't make that advice and lack of support feel any better.

When you're "in it," when you are actively trying to conceive, actively doubting yourself, worried, scared, excited, when you're looking at all the research, learning all the information, the last thing you need is another naysayer.

The best thing for me was to join the message boards, to read success stories, to gain all the information I could. Yes, people are doing it, a lot of people and yes it is working for many, many, many people. Be confident in yourself, have faith, gather your facts so when your mom, your best friend or whoever doubts you says something you will know what you're doing and you will get pregnant.

Choosing A Bank

...can be extremely overwhelming.

- Is it FDA approved?
- Does it cost anything to look at donor information?
- Do the donor profiles provide all the information you are looking for?
  - Genetic Testing
  - Information about the Donor's family
  - Emotional Intelligence information
  - Provide a picture Child/ Adult
- What kind of support does the bank provide?
- Is there a social media group of other people using the services?
  - What is the shipping process like?
  - Is the bank able to be reached easily?

Honestly, I didn't do that much searching around and frankly we didn't need to. Like most things I say, don't over think it. Easier said than done? I know, I know. I am the master of finding something I like and then putting all my efforts into finding something better. There are so many decisions, so many options you have to choose during this journey that once you find a place that is credible, FDA approved and that you like, go with it. One of the main things I've learned during our conception process is to go with my gut.

Facebook Group

I started with pursuing the website of the sperm bank I was considering. Exploring the donors, the information that the bank provided about insemination, who they were as a company. Then I joined the Facebook group for people either actively inseminating or thinking about it. Well, if I wasn't overwhelmed with everything that I didn't know, when I read through the information on the company's website, I was when I got to the group conversation.

The whole thing is a world of acronyms, medical terms, terms made up by whoever felt it necessary at the time. It's like being back in science class when you skipped more than half the classes and have to take an exam. It's ...overwhelming and in the middle of it when you're already worrying, trying to learn as much as you can, stressing the f- out, it can be discouraging.

You don't have to know everything. You don't even have to know half of everything. Even though it's easy to compare how much you don't know compared to how much everyone else seems to know, you'll figure it out. You don't need to memorize acronyms or buy every baby making concoction. When it all comes down to it all you need is to track, track, track and be healthy.

I will say though that the Facebook group was a welcomed friend when I felt confused, a reference guide when I felt lost. While people posted their conquests and their defeats, their worries and their fears, I watched and read and suddenly I didn't feel alone. I also felt like I could and would meet the end goal I dreamed of. I'm not much of an engager on social media, I don't have anyone I know that has been through this, and I'm not one for reaching out. That's why I find it important to share with you. So even if you feel alone, you know you're not.

The Lingo

OMG the abbreviations everyone uses. On every blog, in every group, doctors, nurses, everyone is using these acronyms, letters to explain everything. It's like being the new girl in a middle school cafeteria, it's easy to feel left out.

So not only do you:

> 1. Have to learn everything no one ever taught you about your female organs, reproductive system, how it all works together and how you are going to use all of that to track and plot your conception.

> And

> 2. Figure out where you are getting sperm from, how you are going to pick a donor, etc.

Now you have to learn these secret codes to this secret society so you can then decode everything and try to decipher what it is you actually have to do, what's important, what's not, blah blah blah.

I'm not going to use many of these abbreviations or definitions. I didn't spend too much time on them when I was trying to conceive (which I just learned is this TTC everyone is always writing about.)

Chances are though as you set out on your journey you'll come across them and if you do you'll be empowered in knowing what you know.

AF: Aunt Flow (aka your period.)

BBT: Basal Body Temperature

DPO: Days Past Ovulation

ICI: Intracervical Insemination (what we are talking about, placing sperm close to the cervix.)

ICI-ready Sperm or Unwashed Sperm: It's the sperm in it's natural state with the seminal fluid still in it.

IUI: Intrauterine Insemination (it's the procedure where the sperm is put into the uterus by a professional)

IUI ready Sperm or Washed Sperm: It's sperm that's been separated from the semen.

LH: Luteinizing Hormone (doesn't do a lot in explaining what it actually is or how it is important in you conception story.)

OPK: Ovulation Prediction Kit

TTC: Trying To Conceive

TWW: Two Week Wait (people waiting to see if they got pregnant)

Choosing A Donor

If only finding a partner was this easy. Donors' whole lives are posted up on the internet. Their voice samples, their emotional profiles, their family histories. Just kidding, it's not as easy as it seems, having all the information right there. Basically everything is right there for you to dissect and overthink. Should you get someone that looks like your partner, if you have a partner? And if you don't what do you look at first? I think if I searched multiple sperm banks I could have spent years piddle poddling over what information each company provided and the information they didn't. I could go back and forth about their psychology, their emotional diagrams but as we got deeper into the decision I realized there was more to the selection than just looks and personality.

Anonymous vs. Non Anonymous

I wish my decision was as clear cut as my wife's. She believed that our daughter should, without a doubt, be able to reach out to our donor when she was 18. This is one of the many challenges I never thought I'd face when family planning. Selfish me thought she can't know what she can't know, if I chose anonymous, that would be it, no choice.

But as encouraged by my wife, I thought about it. I travelled down the path that would be our lives, that would be my child's life. Obviously she had to come from somewhere and eventually she will ask about her donor and if I want to live the truth I try to live I'd have to be open, honest and transparent.

We decided to choose a non anonymous donor. There are health benefits to the decision as well but our decision was based primarily on the fact that if she wants to find the man that gave us the most amazing gift we could have been given then no one should have the right to take it away from her. Finding out who you are is hard enough when you're a teenager. I didn't want to make it harder on her, I didn't want her to resent us. With all that being said I'm not jumping for joy with our decision. I'll probably be thinking about whether the day will come when she wants to find out who the donor is for the rest of my life. Until then I'll be content with my decision knowing that we had the best intent for her.

It's a private decision and there's a million different situations you could be in. No matter what you choose, it is the best decision for you.

CMV Status

Cytomegalovirus, sounds scary right? I hear it's very common, people don't usually know they are positive, and it rarely causes problems in people of good health.

So if you meet someone in a bar and you fall head over heels, get married, and start planning a family, chances are you're not going to call the whole thing off should he be CMV positive. Would you even know? Probably not.

I never heard of this virus, and I still don't know very much about it. It was just another thing to worry about when choosing our donors. Another thing to research. Eventually after worrying about things, probably too much, I put myself in the mindset of, if it wouldn't stop me from building a family with the person, had I met them and fallen in love, then I shouldn't spend too much time circling the bush about it.

Our sperm donor decisions

As I mentioned before we tried three times. The first time we chose together, the second and third time I left the decision all up to my wife. I didn't even know who the donor was until I received my positive pregnancy test.

Why?

The first time when we chose the donor he was meticulously picked. I went over every last detail, multiple times. His health, his family's health, his interests. I thought about him before, during and after the inseminations. Was he the right one or was he the wrong one?

He had reported pregnancies, no CMV, we got a high motility count (20 MOTS, IUI ready.) It was what we considered the best of the best sperm and we paid almost $1500 for two vials.

I didn't get pregnant.

The second time my wife picked, I didn't know who it was until I started writing this. The donor was another man we both liked. Well built, healthy, checked all the boxes of a "perfect specimen."

I still didn't get pregnant.

The third donor my wife picked out for us was a guy that we both really liked. He was artistic, creative, but there were a few things that had stopped us from considering him the first time and her the second. He smoked, he didn't have reported pregnancies and his emotional charts read like mine.

Now, I'm a decent fan of myself. That being said I have a tendency to be very hard and critical on myself. I've trained myself throughout my life not to overthink so much, not to dwell so much, and not to take things so personal. So, when looking for donors I tended to direct my search for personality traits that were more like my wife's, traits that could be complementary to my own and wouldn't add to my weaknesses.

I got pregnant.

When it all comes down to it though, much like with this whole process, sometimes it's better just not to over analyze.

Go with instinct, choose what you like, you will be able to guide the way to your future.

Having my wife pick the donor was a great choice for us for reasons I hadn't even thought of before our baby was born. Honestly at the beginning having her choose had a lot to do with stress. After our beautiful baby was born and I looked at her I thought "wow, my wife chose you." If it hadn't been for her we wouldn't have the baby we have now. She picked out our baby, she inseminated me, I'm not sure if it is empowering to her but it has created a huge amount of gratitude inside me for her.

ICI/IUI Sperm

So when you get ready to order your sperm you're faced with the decision, should you order ICI or IUI ready sperm?

ICI (Intra-Cervical Insemination) ready sperm is sperm that isn't washed, it's as it would be if it had come straight out of the source...the penis.

IUI (Intra-Uterine Insemination) ready sperm is washed which means sperm is washed from the seminal fluid. They'll tell you that when you are placing the sperm near the cervix (ICI) you can use either.

So to reiterate you are performing an ICI but you can also use the IUI ready sperm.

Throughout our three attempts we used IUI sperm.

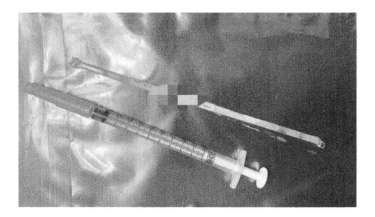

STEP 2: TAKING CONTROL OF TRACKING

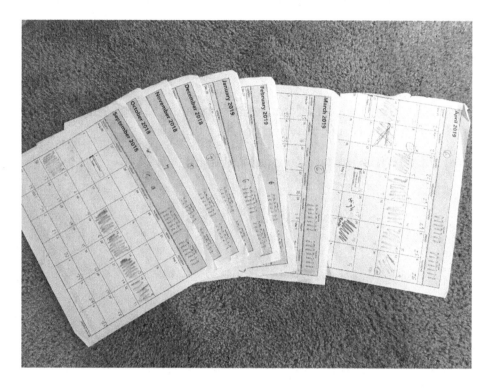

Tracking

• When and how many days is your period?

• How many days is your menstrual cycle? (It starts the first day of your period and ends the day before your next period.)

• When do you ovulate?

• When is your LH surge?

Tracking your period and your menstrual cycle are a lot more cut and dry than finding out when you're ovulating.

You want to inseminate before ovulation.

Basal Body Thermometer

To track my ovulation I used a basal body thermometer every-day, first thing in the morning, before I got out of bed to track my temperature. Did I actually remember every day? Nope. After a few weeks I got a better hang of all the tracking but still forgot every now and then.

For this to go well you have to take your temperature at the same time before you get out of bed, you shouldn't talk or do anything before you take your temperature.

To get a good idea of when you ovulate, track your temperature for a month or two before you draw any conclusions. You defin-itely need to track it from the first day of your cycle to your last before you take a step back and draw any sort of conclusion.

I used graph paper to plot out my temperatures and an app. There are a lot of templates you can print out and most fertility apps will do it too.

<u>What are you looking for?</u>

· The rise in your Basal Body Temperature (BBT) means you have ovulated.

· This means, if you're going to use this method you have to start charting at least 1-2 months before.

· Using your Basal Body Temperature you will be able to tell afterwards when ovulation occured but not ahead of time. So this will help you narrow down your ovulation but it will not help you decide when you need to inseminate.

At times my chart looked as it should, or as everyone said it should online. Other months...it was literally all over the place. Why was it all over the place? Well if I looked it up there were articles that said inconsistencies can be a sign of fertility issues and when I read deeper it didn't seem good for our chances.

If I have fertility issues they couldn't have been too bad considering the outcome. My point? Again this is just a tool, see if it works for you by giving you a closer look at the big picture. A ton of things can go wrong with this, if you didn't get enough sleep, if you drank alcohol, if you got up, talked, etc.

On bad days, when the charts didn't look "as they should," it was enough to send me spiraling because when you're not pregnant it's hard to remember that there is a light at the end of the tunnel. Just because people say something should look like or be a certain way doesn't mean it's the end all be all, it wasn't for me.

L H Strips & Apps

I also used LH strips everyday, twice a day to predict my ovulation. They are tiny test strips of paper. I usually did it twice a day, until I narrowed down my window, once mid morning and in the evening when I got home from work. I used a dixie cup then put the test strip in the cup (I found it neater that way.)

I started tracking in September, our first insemination was in December. At that point I was primarily relying on ovulation apps, my basal body temp and the LH strips to tell me when I was ovulating, then using ovulation tests (OPKs) to narrow the time frame down.

When using LH strips two dark red lines will be your LH peak with your ovulation following in the next 1-2 days. Your LH surge is a good indication of your fertility window and when you want to inseminate.

My opinion? Print out some paper calendars and track everything from the duration of your period, how many days your cycle is, when and how long your LH surge is and how long after do you ovulate. Take your time and track, get to know your body and don't second guess your research on it.

In December we inseminated the 23rd, and 24th. That is when my app instructed me to. That was on day 15 and 16 of my cycle. My ovulation tests did not give me the go ahead but I did it anyway. It didn't work.

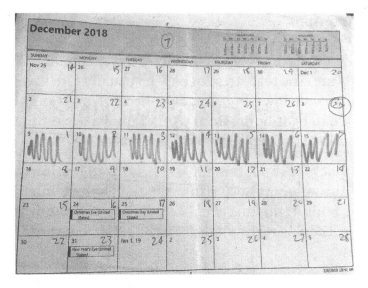

The number circled at the top (7) = Length of period
The red colored days = Days I had my period
The circled 27 = Length of cycle

We were really bummed about it. I thought it was a lot easier, that there was a much bigger window than people made there out to be. When I didn't get pregnant on the first try I was really hard on myself. I took the next two months to track more, to eat better, to take care of me. I got acupuncture, I regularly visited the chiropractor, I used my oils and stuck religiously to the food I had studied to improve my chances. I felt better, a lot better and a lot healthier. Most of all I felt more confident and in control.

March rolled around and we knew what we had to do. We stocked ourselves with four OPKS to use, all the same well known brand. I tested religiously. The problem? One test would say I was high, another would say I wasn't. It was confusing and it psyched me out. At one point two said I was peaking and one didn't. Against my better judgement we inseminated a day before the day I said would be the best.

CD 12
3/23 7:24 pm

CD 14
3/25 7:28 am

CD 15
3/26 7:22 am

CD 15
3/26 6:29 pm

CD 16
3/27 8:13 am

CD 16
3/27 6:57 pm

CD 17
3/28 6:59 am

CD 17
3/28 6:59 am

When we saw I was peaking that morning we called into work and inseminated once on March 27th and twice on March 28th (once in the morning and once at night.) These were the 16th and 17th day of my cycle. Between those times we went out, had lunch, went shopping but the anticipation was still palpable, the stress was there, the hope was there, and the worry of course was ever present. It didn't work. This time I was very discouraged. I felt like a failure. I started doubting my body. I started doubting everything. It took a toll on me, on my wife and I could feel it everyday.

I wasn't a hundred percent confident that time either and that's what I held on to. I knew what was right, didn't I? I knew it was a day too soon. I knew we got too excited, too antsy, that we had jumped the gun.

One more time. That's what we decided on, that we would try one more time and then we would get some outside help, some testing to see if my body was all good, to see if there was anything medically stopping me from getting pregnant.

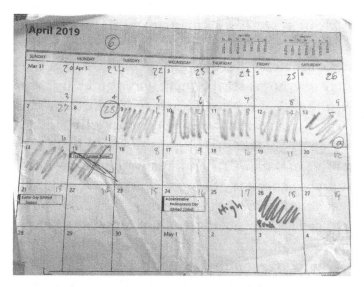

April. We ordered 4 vials of MOT 5, the lowest sperm count we had purchased. We inseminated the night of April 25, the morning and night of the 26th, and the morning of the 27th. Those were the 17th, 18th, and 19th days of my cycle. When my wife got done inseminating me the night of the 26th she said "that was the one, that was the time, you're going to get pregnant.

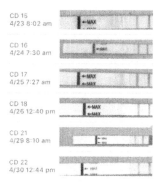

A week before we got the positive pregnancy test (May 12th) we went to see a fertility doctor. One of the best ones around. Sitting in the waiting room was depressing. It was filled with people, sad people, worried people. Lesbians, women alone, and women with men who looked completely beaten down. The journey is tough. I believe it's tough even if you get pregnant the first time, and if you don't, the stress multiplies so rapidly seeping into every orifice of your life. We sat there like every woman in there but besides the worry, there was hope. Maybe there was a quick fix? Maybe nothing was wrong except my poor plotting. Maybe this or maybe that but at least we were taking action. A doctor will know best about what we need to do. Our names got called ,we walked quickly in with our piles of papers in hand, ready to take charge. They did an ultrasound to check my follicles, the nurse said I had plenty of them, I checked that off the list of things that could be wrong. We went in to see the doctor presenting him with all the evidence, all the charting, plotting, everything we had done. Our problem he said? My window couldn't possibly be on the 18th day of my cycle, it's way too late. He packed us with knowledge, the steps we were going to take to get me pregnant. We'd check my fallopian tubes, blood work, this and that, by the time everything was done, within a month or two, I'd be on my way to pregnancy.

Just a couple thousand more dollars for these tests, for some new, better sperm, and the help from this doctor and we would be good to go. We left with hope, we knew the steps we had to take, our next month was outlined perfectly. My gut had been wrong, the apps were right, everything else I wasn't listening to was right.

Wrong.

A week later on Mother's Day we got a positive pregnancy test. The 18th day of my cycle was exactly on point, whether it's too late for most or not it was just right for me. My gut was right, my wife was right when she said that was the one.

I'm not saying don't use this or don't use that, don't see a doctor, don't figure out what's not working if you're not pregnant. What I am saying is use all of your resources, go with what you feel is right. Listen to yourself, don't let things or people bring you down like I did.

According to two popular apps I downloaded on my phone my peak ovulation was about six days before what I calculated my peak to be. It made me confused, sad, it made me second guess myself. I didn't know what to trust. I wanted to trust myself but the app seemed so much easier to trust, everyone uses it right?

It was definitely a good tool and I would recommend using the apps to track everything too. It's great at the beginning and even at the end. The most important thing though for me? Is that I trusted myself.

During my whole journey I used LH tests, everyday. I used an app where I took a picture of the LH test everyday and it would electronically calculate my peak ovulation...it worked as an additional tool but I wouldn't rely on it solely. We also taped all the LH strips to paper and tried to track it that way.

Another app we used to track ovulation worked as far as giving us a window of about when I would ovulate but the peak was off.

It makes sense that apps alone can't tell you when you're peaking, it's your body, right? All of these tools were useful and when used together, I think, they all help each other help you find out what exactly your body is doing.

How long should you track for? I'd track for at least 3 months if you are regular. The days of my cycle varied, my LH test strips were all over the place sometimes... same with the length of my periods, etc. For me, the five months of hardcore tracking with apps, ovulation tests and tracking my cycle was key.

The short:

• Track with LH strips, a print out calendar and ovulation test predictors (OPKs) for 3 months to narrow down your window.

• When the LH strips show two dark red lines it is your peak. It occurs for about 1-2 days before ovulation

• Your LH surge usually lasts for about 12 to 24 hours. That is why you are tracking so you know if it is longer or shorter.

• After ovulation you only have 12-24 hours for your egg to be fertilized. You want to narrow down that window.

• We inseminated 6 hours after first indication of the LH surge then 6 hours after then 6 hours and about 12 hours after.

• If you have 2 vials go for 12 hour after then 24 if it makes sense with your tracking. If you get 3 do 12, 24 and 36.

What to Know:
When is your LH surge every month?
How long does it last?

Notes:

The first day of your period is the first day of your cycle.

The last day of your cycle is the day before your period.

The number of days between the first day of your period and the day before your next period is how long your cycle is.

Ovulation usually happen 12-36 hours after your LH surge.

There's different lengths of cycles, there are different lengths in LH surges, and different lengths between LH surges and ovulation.

You need to track and understand your body and your cycle and adjust accordingly.

Tools I Used

LH testing strips

Small dixie cups for LH tests

Digital Ovulation Tests (4)
Fertility Tracker Apps (3)
Paper calendars, pens and markers

STEP 3: TAKING CHARGE OF YOUR HEALTH

Food

Finding food that works for me and my needs has always been a hobby of mine. I find joy in researching herbs, spices, and everyday grocery goods that will help me along my journey whether that's sleeplessness, a cold, or fertility. I'm not a health nut, I'm not a vegetarian or vegan, I don't often restrict myself and I do give into to sour gummy snacks (my weakness) every so often.

I do think about what I eat and sometimes I think myself through almost a whole bag of potato chips leaving just enough to feel good that at least I didn't eat the whole bag. I choose whole foods as much as I can, not because they are healthier, but because I feel better over all.

Eating, when you put your mind into it, is something relatively simple you can do to help yourself with fertility. You can feel good knowing you are personally taking charge, making good food choices and taking control of your situation.

Now, I'm not a nutritionist, at all. I'm not thin and I would not say I am in the best shape. I can say though that I try to incorporate healthy and helpful food decisions into my everyday life.

I threw myself into the research of foods I should be eating to help conceive, to make myself more fertile, to regulate my periods and above all else (in my opinion) to feel confident in myself and capable inside my body. As I mixed and matched foods, planned, prepared and followed my meals, planning relatively close I saw an enormous change in my body and the way I felt.

The feeling was strange because I wasn't starving myself, I was actually eating a ton more than I usually do. It was strange because the food I was eating wasn't so different from my regular diet. All I can say I guess is that it was the right amount to do the right things.

The changes I saw and felt

My sex drive

All of a sudden I felt sexy, for a while, with all the stress of what was going on in my life in addition to the daunting task of our insemination I had lost that tingle in my vagina that happens at arousal. Before I had had quite the sex drive but through time and stresses it went away. When I started to eat the things that I read help conception it was back! I couldn't believe it, I felt great, I felt in the mood and ready to go.

My vaginal fluid. I wasn't a big tracker of my vaginal fluid before we got into the insemination process. It was there sometimes and other times it wasn't. Sometimes it was enough to leak through my pants but also over the years the variety of amount and textures kind of went away so for the most part I had thin discharge with no smell. Well, a few weeks into my change of diet I was noticing the discharge transitions all the trackers told me I should be looking out for. What I ate mattered. I didn't think about how it could change these factors that seemed like obstacles that kept me from where I wanted to go.

Your Cervical Mucus

It's a good indicator of your fertility.
Cervical mucus helps the semen get to where it's going.
You are looking for clear slippery mucus that looks like and feels like egg whites, that indicates your most fertile time.

Energy and Mood

I was eating a lot. Maybe even more than anyone would say was healthy. But I never felt better. I felt more optimistic and energetic. I felt like everything was coming together. What I ate helped me get out of bed which made me be able to exercise more which made me feel even better.

Body

And of course besides everything else I listed, above all else, my body started to feel and look better. I wasn't thinner or losing weight, the texture of my skin was noticeably more rejuvenated. I was fuller and my skin was tighter. I'm a big lotion girl and all of a sudden, I didn't need to apply so much. Through food you can feed your body to be whatever you want it to be.

It's really hard to eat healthy, or to eat balanced. For some people it's hard to eat at all and for others it's hard to not indulge in all the fun foods out there. All I did is the best I could do. I educated myself in what the best foods to heighten my chances were. I put together lists, I gathered appropriate ingredients that I thought I could combine to create meals with the most amount of bang for my buck, so to speak. At the end of the day all anyone can do is their best. Schedules are hard, creating a routine is challenging but hopefully the following digging I did, the lists and recipes I included can help make your life a little easier.

Everyday while I was trying to conceive I'd eat a hardboiled egg in the morning, a little later I would eat yogurt with a high milkfat percentage with some oats mixed in, honey, berries and a handfull of walnuts. Regularly I would bring a smoothie in with me to work. I'd eat an avocado daily. Other things I used to snack on were walnuts and roasted garlic, kale chips, pineapple, clementines, and bananas. For lunch I'd eat quinoa salad or stuffed peppers. Dinner is always a conundrum in our household, meaning a big mess and a giant lack of decisions. SO long story short I always tried to have a good source of protein (salmon, steak, chicken) with rich dark greens (bok choy, asparagus) My favorite desert was Cocao chia seed pudding.

<u>What I Ate</u>

☐ Blueberries ☐ Quinoa ☐Eggs ☐ Black Beans
☐ High Fat Greek Yogurt ☐ Walnuts
☐ Sweet Potatoes ☐ Black Beans☐ Chia Seeds
☐ Salmon ☐ Leafy Greens ☐ Maca Powder
☐ Sweet Potatos ☐ Salmon ☐ Avocados ☐ Asparagus
☐ Lentils ☐ Clementines☐ Grapefruit ☐ Tumeric
☐ Ginger☐ Chickpeas☐ Honey ☐ Oats

Acupuncture/Chiropractor

As we were preparing to start our family I really started taking charge of issues I'd been dealing with for quite sometime, including my pain. I've always had bad back pain that rippled through my body. At times it was completely debilitating, it made me irritable, it robbed me of my sleep. I dealt with it throughout my early 20s and as it got worse I let it consume me more. I felt really bad for myself and I think that had the biggest impact on me. Not only did I have back pain, I had pain that would travel throughout my body, maybe it stemmed from my back, maybe it didn't, but there were times, out of nowhere I could do nothing except cry.

So when we talked about inseminating and preparing for the whole process I started to take control of myself. The first step was seeing an acupuncturist for my pain and then after my pain lessened and we started ICI I looked into it more for fertility.

I didn't use it during our first attempt but the two other times I went regularly. That included the recommended times (around day 5 of your menstruation, the day of ovulation and around implantation which is from 6-12 days after ovulation.)

To take charge of my pain situation I also started to see a chiropractor. Initially, I went two times a week (it was extreme because my pain was extreme.) I did that for six weeks during my last two times inseminating.

I honestly believe if it weren't for my acupuncturist and my chiropractor I wouldn't have been successful so quickly.

This whole thing takes a toll on you so the less you have

going on elsewhere in your body and in your life the better. Tie up those loose ends, let go of resentments, take care of your health, your mind, and your soul. No, your fertility doctor won't tell you that and you probably won't see it top any lists on how to boost your chances to conceive but the better you feel mentally and physically the better your body will be at carrying out what you want it to do.

Having these resources has definitely been an asset to me throughout my pregnancy too.

Essential Oils

I've always loved essential oils as an added aid to help me down whatever path I was headed.

Since I'm not rich and oils are pretty expensive, I invested in four:

- Clary Sage- Balances hormones, enhances libido
- Rose Otto- Regulates menstrual cyle, enhances cervical mucus
- Geranium- Regulates hormones
- Lavender- Regulates menstrual cycles, relaxation, lowers cortisol levels

Every night before bed I prepared a small concoction a few drops of each in the diffuser next to bed that way all night I would be filled, my body prepped, for fertility.

In the mornings before work I'd dab a drop or two of geranium and rose otto on my wrists. At lunch I'd put some Clary Sage above my lip so I would breath it in all afternoon.

Massages with the oils are always relaxing too!

<u>Tools I used</u>
Clary Sage
Rose Otto
Geranium
Lavender
Small diffuser

Extras

<u>Mucinex</u>

The last month we inseminated, the successful time, I started taking Mucinex everyday starting 5 days before I predicted my fertile window to be.

Why?
I read multiple places that it helped thin out your cervical mucus and made it easier for the sperm to travel to my egg.

<u>Frankincense</u>

I burned frankincense incense often before, during and after our insemination. I usually burned it while I was doing my morning stretches or after I had gotten acupuncture.

Why?
Frankincense is believed to have a lot of health benefits that can also aid in conception. It balances hormones which helps regulate your menstrual cycle, it's said to tone your uterus and aid implantation.

Everyday Routine

Morning
Took my temperature using a Basal thermometer
Prenatal pill
Folic Acid
Fish Oil
Breakfast
> Yogurt Bowl
> Hardboiled egg

Walk
Stretch and Meditate
Burned frankincense
Head to work

Mid Morning
Smoothie
Citrus fruit (clementines, grapefruit, etc)
Avocado (dress up with lemon)

Lunch
LH strip test
Quinoa Salad

Afternoon To Evening
Roasted Garlic Cloves
Dinner
High protein, leafy greens
LH strip test

Nighttime
Filled diffuser with oils
Went to bed at a reasonable time

STEP 4: THE EXECUTION

Insemination

How romantic, how intimate it is to be able to inseminate at home. I guess it'd be nice if this glamorized version of the whole situation was true. Some of the people who actually asked how we did it were fascinated in the romanticized version of it all. Was it romantic? Meh, in theory. Of course we are lucky to have this option and I am so thankful my wife and I were able to do it on our own at home. Was it like the real deal? No. Was it sexual? Not at all. Unless you call me micromanaging the whole situation, legs spread, asking a million questions, my wife jabbing the speculum nervously inside of me in a quest to find the cervix, a hot and steamy affair.

You're likely not a doctor. Your partner...probably not one either but if you or they are, good for you. For the rest of us, it's probably a bit unnerving, unsettling, scary, strange.

My suggestion, if you do have a partner, have them use the speculum to exam the whole situation before the actual insemination process. Get used to a plastic or in my case a metal device being manipulated in your private area by someone who isn't trained in doing so. It's not like being at the doctors office getting examined. It's like if your partner was to take the speculum and open you up, exactly what it is.

The first few times we did it it was strenuous to say the least. I was scared, my vagina was scared and both of us tensed up, the more we did it the more relaxed and accustomed I got to the whole thing and relaxed in my unrelaxing situation.

There were many times I was on the bed, legs spread getting inseminated asking myself how did I get here, what a great indie movie this would make, the fights and arguments, the disagreements we had before, during, and after the inseminations of sperm we ordered online. Could anyone imagine this? Could I?

As I've gone through this pregnancy and getting ready for the birth, one of the biggest most useful tools I've gained was the ability to go elsewhere. Enjoy the process if you can and if you can't meditate, practice getting out of your head. Not only will it relax your body and your mind it will create positivity and you will get pregnant.

<u>To inseminate or not to inseminate?</u>

I think the biggest thing that screwed with our minds was when to inseminate. You have your vials of sperm you've spent a lot of money on, you have months of built up hope and dreams, and you don't want to do it too early but you can't miss it either.

Take a deep breath.

We had our success when we inseminated 4 times with the lowest sperm count. We inseminated 6 hours after my peak and then every six hours for two more times and the last we waited 12 hours. If you have two vials they say to do 12 hours after your peak and then 24 hours. If you have one do it 24 hours after.

What worked for us

After burning some frankincense and getting into a relaxing mood, all while of course thawing out our sperm for the recommended 15 minutes, my wife got the sperm ready with the syringe, I sat at the edge of our bed (like I would at the OBGYN) legs spread. My wife then inserted the speculum and opened it up, as uncomfortable as it is, I found waiting a minute or two with it in helped me get used to the feeling more and relax. Using the speculum as sort of a viewfinder my wife searched for the cervix and when she found it she put the syringe as far as she could get it and as close as she could get it to my cervix. The time she knew she got me pregnant she said my cervix was open, like it hadn't been before.

For about an hour each time I held my legs above my head, most often and the time I got pregnant I'd prop my legs against the wall and placed pillows under my butt. After that I put in a soft cup and went about my business with the soft cup in for about 8 hours.

Preseed

I didn't use it. In my mind mixing sperm with anything else just makes for a more convoluted process.

Tools I Used

Speculum

Soft Cups

Frankincense Incense

Implantation and The Two Week Wait

The two attempts before our successful month I was sure I was pregnant. I was nauseous, my breasts were bigger, I felt so...pregnant ...except I didn't even know what pregnancy felt like. Whether I had made myself have the symptoms that I had looked up online or not, I wasn't pregnant. It's a difficult time, the hardest. I never waited two weeks before taking a pregnancy test, I always got bummed before it was my time to get bummed. Even the third, successful month I bummed myself out because the nurse at the fertility office said they couldn't see anything, but it would be too early to tell anyway.

The early symptoms of pregnancy are many times what I felt before I got my period but my imagination also played a decent part in me having these early pregnancy symptoms. I feel like a built myself up the first two months, my wife and I sat feeling my breasts, they are definitely bigger, my need to devour a whole bag of gummy worms...definitely a pregnancy craving and not my lack of self control. Every time I peed more than once an hour, every cramp, every craving thrilled me because I was sure I was pregnant...and when I got my period, I was devastated and I felt like I failed.

The third try I was extremely discouraged, I was down on myself, I was down on the process. The state of my mind, my relationship with my wife and the people close to me, and my overall wellbeing was shit.

I kept on though. My mind said I wasn't pregnant that this was the same thing I had been through before, the only difference? I didn't feel nauseous, my breasts didn't feel tender. I was so not pregnant I didn't have any of the made up symptoms I had had before.

I did the same things I had been doing. Eating, I was eating all the things there were to eat to increase implantation chances.

- Almonds on everything
- Pineapple, everyday
- Garlic, garlic and more garlic
- Avocados, Everyday
- Hard boiled eggs

I took my prenatal, folic acid, went to the acupuncturist and the chiropractor.

We went to see the fertility doctor I talked about earlier and when he said there was no way I was pregnant because my timing was off I was sure I was not pregnant. But guess what, I was!

On Mother's Day, 7 days after I was supposed to have my period we tested. I couldn't believe it.

The most important thing

The most important thing is that you believe in yourself, that you don't give up, that you know you will get pregnant. After you get pregnant you will have the life you have always wanted. You can have everything.

There were a lot of times where I was so stressed, so discouraged.

It's a journey and the journey isn't always easy but it is worth it.

I want to be there for you in every and any way I can. If you have any questions, if you feel like I have left out anything please don't hesitate to reach out on Instagram at @alittlelooseleaf.

APPENDIX

Recipes

Yogurt Bowl

1 Cup Yogurt

½ Frozen Blueberries

2 Teaspoons Cinnamon

Walnuts

Drizzle of Honey

½ Cup of Oats

Pour oats in bowl

Lay yogurt on top

Add blueberries and walnuts (to preference)

Sprinkle cinnamon on top

And drizzle with honey

Super Smoothie

1 tbsp Maca Powder

½ Cup Frozen Berries

4oz Coconut Water

4oz Almond Milk

Ginger

1 tbsp Flax Seeds

Handful of Spinach

1 tbsp of Coconut Oil

1 Banana

⅓ Cup Ice

Combine all ingredients in a blender

Quinoa Salad

1 Cup Quinoa

1 Can Black Beans

2 Teaspoons of Cayenne Pepper

2 Cloves of Garlic (chopped or minced)

¼ Cup of Olive Oil

¼ Cup Lemon/Lime Juice

2 Cups Arugala

1 Cup Halved Cherry Tomatoes

2 Green Onions Sliced

Sesame Seeds
Feta Cheese
Salt and Pepper
Cook Quinoa
Mix Olive Oil, Garlic, Cayenne Pepper, Lemon/Lime Juice
Mix cooked Quinoa with Black Beans, Arugula, Cherry Tomatoes, Green Onions.
Top with Dressing
Add Feta Cheese, Salt, Pepper, and Sesame Seeds

Tracking Calendars

Number top left = Ovulation Cycle Day
Red circle bottom left = Menstrual Cycle
☆ = Insemination (left = day, right = night)
A = Acupuncture

September

Sunday	Monday	Tuesday	Wednesday	Thursday	Friday	Saturday
						1
2	3	4	5	6	7	8
9	10	11	12 1 ○	13 2 ○	14 3 ○	15 4 ○
16 5 ○	17 6	18 7	19 8	20 9	21 10	22 11
23 12	24 13	25 14	26 15	27 16	28 17	29 18

October

Sunday	Monday	Tuesday	Wednesday	Thursday	Friday	Saturday
30 19	**1** 20	**2** 21	**3** 22	**4** 23	**5** 24	**6** 25
7 26	**8** 27	**9** 28	**10** 29	**11** 1 ○	**12** 2 ○	**13** 3 ○
14 4 ○	**15** 5 ○	**16** 6 ○	**17** 7 ○	**18** 8	**19** 9	**20** 10
21 11	**22** 12	**23** 13	**24** 14	**25** 15	**26** 16	**27** 17
28 18	**29** 19	**30** 20	**31** 21			

November

Sunday	Monday	Tuesday	Wednesday	Thursday	Friday	Saturday
				1 22	**2** 23	**3** 24
4 25	**5** 26	**6** 27	**7** 28	**8** 29	**9** 30	**10** 31
11 32	**12** 1 ○	**13** 2 ○	**14** 3 ○	**15** 4 ○	**16** 5 ○	**17** 6
18 7	**19** 8	**20** 9	**21** 10	**22** 11	**23** 12	**24** 13
25 14	**26** 15	**27** 16	**28** 17	**29** 18	**30** 19	

December

Sunday	Monday	Tuesday	Wednesday	Thursday	Friday	Saturday
						1 20
2 21	**3** 22	**4** 23	**5** 24	**6** 25	**7** 26	**8** 27
9 1 ⊙	**10** 2 ⊙	**11** 3 ⊙	**12** 4 ⊙	**13** 5 ⊙	**14** 6 ⊙	**15** 7 ⊙
16 8	**17** 9	**18** 10	**19** 11	**20** 12	**21** 13	**22** 14
23 15	**24** 16 ☆	**25** 17 ☆	**26** 18	**27** 19	**28** 20	**29** 21

Delivered: December 28
Quantity: 2 Vials
MOT 20
Type: IUI Ready

January

Sunday	Monday	Tuesday	Wednesday	Thursday	Friday	Saturday
30 22	**31** 23	**1** 24	**2** 25	**3** 26	**4** 27	**5** 28
6 29	**7** 1 ○	**8** 2 ○	**9** 3 ○	**10** 4 ○	**11** 5 ○	**12** 6 ○
13 7	**14** 8	**15** 9	**16** 10	**17** 11	**18** 12	**19** 13
20 14	**21** 15	**22** 16	**23** 17	**24** 18	**25** 19	**26** 20
27 21	**28** 22	**29** 23	**30** 24	**31** 25		

February

Sunday	Monday	Tuesday	Wednesday	Thursday	Friday	Saturday
					1 26	**2** 27
3 28	**4** 29	**5** 30	**6** 31	**7** 32	**8** 33	**9** 34
10 1 ○	**11** 2 ○	**12** 3 ○	**13** 4 ○	**14** 5 ○	**15** 6 ○	**16** 7
17 8	**18** 9	**19** 10	**20** 11	**21** 12	**22** 13	**23** 14
24 15	**25** 16	**26** 17	**27** 18	**28** 19		

March

Sunday	Monday	Tuesday	Wednesday	Thursday	Friday	Saturday
					1 20	**2** 21
3 22	**4** 23	**5** 24	**6** 25	**7** 26	**8** 27	**9** 28
10 29	**11** 30	**12** 1 ○	**13** 2 ○	**14** 3 ○	**15** 4 ○	**16** 5 ○ A
17 6 ○	**18** 7	**19** 8	**20** 9	**21** 10	**22** 11	**23** 12 A
24 13	**25** 14	**26** 15	**27** 16 ☆	**28** 17 ☆ ☆	**29** 18	**30** 19

Delivered: March 27
Quantity: 3 Vials MOT 10
Type: IUI Ready
Inseminated: 03/27

April

Sunday	Monday	Tuesday	Wednesday	Thursday	Friday	Saturday
31 20	1 21	2 22	3 23	4 24	5 25	6 26 A
7 27	8 28	9 1 ○	10 2 ○	11 3 ○	12 4 ○	13 5 ○ A
14 6 ○	15 7	16 8	17 9	18 10	19 11	20 12 A
21 13	22 14	23 15	24 16 A	25 17	26 18 ☆ ☆ A	27 19 ☆ ☆
28 20	29 21	30 22				

Delivered: April 24
Quantity: 4 Vials MOT 5
Type: IUI Ready

May

Sunday	Monday	Tuesday	Wednesday	Thursday	Friday	Saturday
			1 23	2 24	3 25	4 26 A
5 27	6 28	7 1	8 2	9 3	10 4	11 5 A
12 6 Positive!	13	14	15	16	17	18
19	20	21	22	23	24	25
26	27	28	29	30	31	

My "Get" List

Essential Oil List

☐ Lavender
☐ Clary Sage
☐ Rose Otto
☐ Geranium
☐ Diffuser

Tracking List

☐ LH testing strips
☐ Small dixie cups for LH tests
☐ Digital Ovulation Tests (4)
☐ Fertility Tracker Apps (3)
☐ Paper calendars, pens and markers

Insemination List

☐ Speculum
☐ Soft Cups
☐ Frankincense Incense

Other
☐ Prenatal Pill
☐ Folic Acid Pill
☐ Frankincense

Things you Should Know About You

- When and how many days is your period?

- How many days is your menstrual cycle?

- When do you ovulate?

- When is your LH surge every month?

- How long does it last?

Now go and get you pregnant!

EPILOGUE

The journey to conception can be long, it can be stressful but it is worth it.

If you have any questions, want to share your story, or just want to chat feel free to reach out to me on Instagram at:

@alittlelooseleaf

Made in the USA
Middletown, DE
24 September 2020

20493289R00036